WHERE'S WALLY?
Simply Sensational
ACTIVITY BOOK

Based on the characters created by

MARTIN HANDFORD

WALKER BOOKS
AND SUBSIDIARIES
LONDON • BOSTON • SYDNEY • AUCKLAND

HI THERE, WALLY-WATCHERS

I'M JUST OFF ON ANOTHER ASTOUNDING ADVENTURE, SO FOLLOW ME AND FIND ME THROUGH THE PAGES OF THIS BOOK. WHAT A GREAT JOURNEY YOU HAVE AHEAD OF YOU – INTO THE FUTURE, BACK TO THE PAST, UP ON THE MOON AND DOWN UNDER THE SEA.

AS WELL AS FINDING ME IN EVERY PICTURE, O FAITHFUL FOLLOWERS OF WALLY, THERE ARE AN AMAZING NUMBER OF THINGS TO DO ON THE WAY - GAMES TO PLAY, TONGUETWISTERS TO SAY, RIDDLES TO SOLVE AND FACTS TO LEARN. I KNOW I'LL DISCOVER LOTS OF NEW FRIENDS ON MY JOURNEY, BUT CAN YOU HELP ME SPOT A COUPLE OF OLD ONES? WENDA APPEARS ONCE AND YOU SHOULD SEE WIZARD WHITEBEARD AND WOOF TWICE. AND CAN YOU COLLECT 3 SCROLLS? KEEP AN EYE OPEN FOR ODLAW, AND A SMALL RED AND WHITE WALLY FLAG.

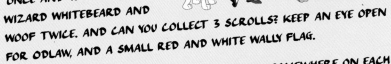

THERE IS ONE MORE TASK TO TELL YOU ABOUT. SOMEWHERE ON EACH PAGE IS A CHARACTER OR OBJECT THAT BELONGS TO ANOTHER SCENE IN THE BOOK. CAN YOU SPOT THE MISFITS AND FIND WHICH PICTURES THEY COME FROM?

THE ANSWERS TO ALL THE RIDDLES ARE IN THE BACK, BUT NO CHEATING! AND IF YOU ARE NOT TOO EXHAUSTED, EACH PAGE HAS ITS OWN CHECK LIST OF 10 THINGS TO FIND.

WOW WALLY-WATCHERS, WHAT ARE YOU WAITING FOR? GET READY, GET STEADY AND GET STARTED ON A SIMPLY SENSATIONAL ADVENTURE!

Wally

MONSTER CARNIVAL

DID YOU KNOW?

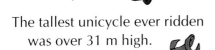

The tallest unicycle ever ridden was over 31 m high.

One of the longest journeys ever undertaken on a unicycle was 1450 km, from Land's End to John o' Groats.

THINGS TO DO

Here are 4 pieces of picture. 2 belong to this page and 2 come from somewhere else in the book. Can you find exactly where?

A   B   C   D

Why couldn't the bicycle stand up for itself?

Because it was two-tyred.

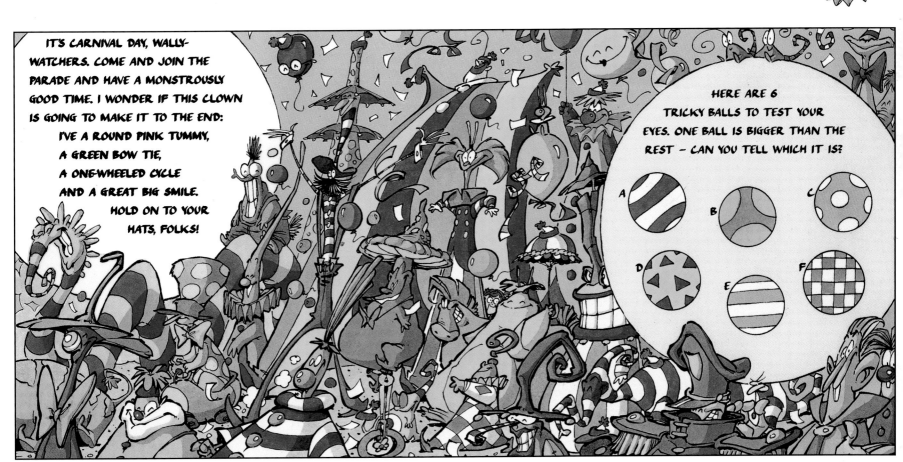

IT'S CARNIVAL DAY, WALLY-WATCHERS. COME AND JOIN THE PARADE AND HAVE A MONSTROUSLY GOOD TIME. I WONDER IF THIS CLOWN IS GOING TO MAKE IT TO THE END:
I'VE A ROUND PINK TUMMY,
A GREEN BOW TIE,
A ONE-WHEELED CYCLE
AND A GREAT BIG SMILE.
HOLD ON TO YOUR HATS, FOLKS!

HERE ARE 6 TRICKY BALLS TO TEST YOUR EYES. ONE BALL IS BIGGER THAN THE REST – CAN YOU TELL WHICH IT IS?

A   B   C   D   E   F

FABULOUS FOOD

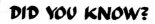

DID YOU KNOW?

The largest ever continuous sausage was made in England in 1988 and measured 21.12 km.

The biggest tomato on record weighed 3.51 kg.

The stems and leaves of a tomato plant are toxic and could make you extremely ill if you ate them.

THINGS TO DO

Here are 6 fruit and vegetable circle puzzles. To solve each one start at any corner and read clockwise or anticlockwise.

R O O T T E E B	C R E U B C U M	M A T O O T S E	M M O U O S H R	T A T O O P S E	S H E I S D A R

Which of these can be seen in the picture?

What vegetable needs a plumber?

A leek.

HERE IS A FABULOUS FANTASY FOR ANY FAMISHED WALLY-WATCHERS, BUT EVEN IF YOU FIND SOMETHING TASTY IT IS QUITE LIKELY TO GET UP AND WALK OFF YOUR PLATE. CAN YOU SPOT THIS SHY VEGETABLE?

IT'S TRYING TO HIDE
BUT IS EASILY SEEN,
IT'S ORANGE AND POPULAR
AT HALLOWE'EN.

IN ALL THIS CHAOS SOMEONE HAS BROKEN A PLATE. MOST BITS HAVE BEEN STUCK BACK TOGETHER BUT CAN YOU FIND THE LAST 2 PIECES FROM THE 4 BELOW?

A

B

C

D

E

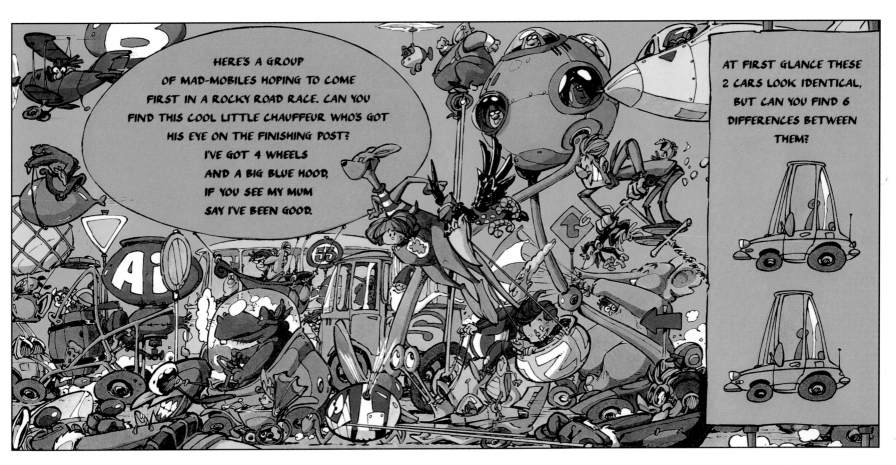

CRAZY CARS

DID YOU KNOW?

If you could travel round the world in a car it would take you 453 hours, travelling at 55 mph. That's over 2 1/2 weeks.

In 1930 Charles Creighton and James Hargis drove their car all the way from New York to Los Angeles in reverse without stopping. They then drove all the way back in reverse. The whole trip took 42 days.

One of the longest traffic jams ever stretched 176 km between Lyon and Paris, France.

THINGS TO DO

How many words can you make out of

JUGGERNAUT

10, quite good; 20, good; over 30, simply sensational!

Why did the motorist drive her car in reverse?

Because she knew the rules of the road backwards.

ONE GLIMPSE OF THE SUN AND EVERYONE'S OUT FOR SOME SENSATIONAL SEASIDE FUN. THIS PLACE IS SO POPULAR EVEN THE DOLPHINS HAVE TO QUEUE UP TO SWIM. CAN YOU SEE EMERALDA, THE GREEN FOREST WOMAN, HAVING A WHALE OF A TIME, AND WHAT ABOUT THE CRAZY MAN DRIVING HIS JET-SKI UP THE WAVE?

I'M HAVING A SWELL TIME, BUT I'M NOT SURE THIS FURRY FRIEND ENJOYS THE WATER:

I'M HERE ON THE ROLLERS
BY DRACULA LED,
I'D MUCH RATHER BE
AT HOME IN YOUR BED.

HERE IS A COLLECTION OF THINGS THAT WALLY FOUND ON THE BEACH. CAN YOU SPOT WHICH 2 OBJECTS ARE THE ODD ONES OUT?

SURFER'S PARADISE

DID YOU KNOW?

The first recorded surfer was Lt James King, who surfed off Hawaii Island in 1779.

It is possible to ride a wave for 1700 m in Matancha Bay, Mexico.

About 70% of the world's total surface is covered by water.

THINGS TO DO

Get from one ocean to another by following the instructions:

Start with	A T L A N T I C
Change all Ts to Is	_ _ _ _ _ _ _ _
Change both As to Cs	_ _ _ _ _ _ _ _
Remove the first I	_ _ _ _ _ _ _
Make the first C a P	_ _ _ _ _ _ _
Change the L to an A	_ _ _ _ _ _ _
Swap the N and the first I	_ _ _ _ _ _ _
Change the N to an F	_ _ _ _ _ _ _

What's the best cure for seasickness? uʍop pooɟ ɹnoʎ ʇlog

SHOPPING SPREE

DID YOU KNOW?

The first supermarket was opened in 1916 in Memphis, Tennessee in America. It was called the Piggly Wiggly store!

The largest cheese ever weighed over 18 kg.

In 1989 a team of workers built a whole stadium out of two million empty tin cans. It took 18,000 hours.

THINGS TO DO

Crack the code and find out what Wally was looking for in the shop. The first letter is underlined.

2 cakes	1 biscuit	5 apricots	5 apricots
	3 onions	2 sherberts	2 cakes
	5 oranges	4 lemons	7 haddock
		5 apricots	7 sausages
		4 lemons	
		4 apples	
		2 cakes	
		3 potatoes	
		7 sausages	

What's the study of shopping called?

Buy-ology.

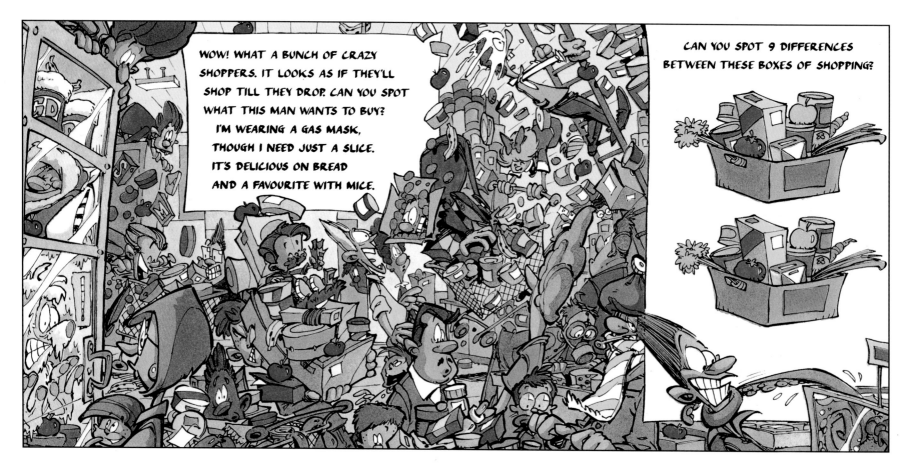

WOW! WHAT A BUNCH OF CRAZY SHOPPERS. IT LOOKS AS IF THEY'LL SHOP TILL THEY DROP. CAN YOU SPOT WHAT THIS MAN WANTS TO BUY? I'M WEARING A GAS MASK, THOUGH I NEED JUST A SLICE. IT'S DELICIOUS ON BREAD AND A FAVOURITE WITH MICE.

CAN YOU SPOT 9 DIFFERENCES BETWEEN THESE BOXES OF SHOPPING?

MOON WALKING

DID YOU KNOW?

It would take a car travelling at 60 mph 175 years to reach the sun.

Most planets, including the Earth, spin from west to east, left to right, clockwise, but Venus spins from east to west.

When astronauts are weightless in space their muscles stretch slightly, making them a little taller.

THINGS TO DO

Here are the names of 8 space operations. Can you find them all in the grid?

VOYAGER   APOLLO

ATLANTIS   EXPLORER   MERCURY

SPUTNIK   NASA   DISCOVERY

Read the remaining letters from left to right on every line and you will learn another fascinating space fact.

N	E	V	O	Y	A	G	E	R	I
L	A	N	R	M	S	T	R	O	N
M	G	A	W	A	S	T	H	E	F
E	I	S	R	S	T	M	A	N	O
R	N	A	T	L	A	N	T	I	S
C	D	I	S	C	O	V	E	R	Y
U	T	H	A	P	O	L	L	O	E
R	E	R	O	L	P	X	E	M	O
Y	K	I	N	T	U	P	S	O	N

What do you call a crazy spaceman? *An astronut.*

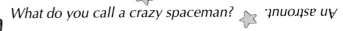

BALL SPORTS

DID YOU KNOW?

There was a game played in Mexico in the tenth century called Po-ta-Pok. It was very like basketball, but if a player managed to shoot the ball through the ring he or she would win all the spectators' clothing!

Basketball players are often very tall. The tallest was Manute Bol who played for the Washington Bullets. He measured 2.30 m.

THINGS TO DO

Here are 8 jumbled sports. Can you unjumble them and find the odd one out?

TOLOFABL   SITNEN

STELLABBAK

FLOG   WIGMINMS   KONORES

BEALSLAB   LOVELLYLAB

What does a ball do when it stops rolling?

It looks round.

WOW! I'M NOT SURE THESE CRAZY BASKETBALL PLAYERS HAVE QUITE MASTERED ALL THE RULES, BUT THEY'RE HAVING A BALL ANYWAY. THERE ARE SEVERAL UNSUITABLE BITS OF EQUIPMENT ON THE COURT. CAN YOU FIND THIS ONE?
THIS BAT USUALLY HITS A LITTLE WHITE BALL, BUT THE HOLE IN THE MIDDLE IS NO GOOD AT ALL.

WHICH OF THESE BALLS SHOULD NOT BE PLAYED WITH BY HAND?

WELL, HERE'S A BIT OF MONKEY BUSINESS. HE HAS JUST DROPPED IN TO SAY HALLO – BUT HE DOESN'T KNOW HIS OWN STRENGTH. CAN YOU SPOT THIS POOR MAN WHO LOOKS VERY CROSS AT BEING DISTURBED?

HE'S ON THE TOP FLOOR
AND LOOKS PRETTY MAD,
HE'S MISSING THE DINNER
HE THOUGHT HE ONCE HAD.
PHEW! THIS WAS AN EARTH-SHATTERING EXPERIENCE.

WHICH SILHOUETTE EXACTLY MATCHES THE FEARLESS FLIER BELOW?

A   B   C   D

MONKEY MISCHIEF

DID YOU KNOW?

Monkeys and apes are different. A monkey has a long tail and an ape has such a short tail it cannot be seen.

The tallest gorilla measured 1.88 m high.

The smallest known monkey is the Pygmy Marmoset, which is about 14 cm long.

THINGS TO DO

In the letter maze below there are 10 animals – 5 across and 5 down. Pick either letter from each pair and find a hidden animal, reading across each line once. Then take the leftover letters and read the animals down.

```
H T   C I   P G   E S   R H
M O   O H   A U   H S   E Y
R Z   E I   N B   R E   A E
S C   A M   D M   E E   L N
W E   H P   A A   P L   A E
```

How does a monkey cook his toast?

On a gorilla.

HELP THIS MARTIAN PICK UP A BURGER AND LEMONADE AND TAKE THEM TO HIS FRIEND.

FLYING SAUCERS

DID YOU KNOW?

People have been spotting UFOs (Unidentified Flying Objects) since the thirteenth century.

Most UFOs can be explained away as clouds or reflections from stars, but not all of them. In 1971 2 Americans claimed to have been captured and examined by aliens on board a UFO.

THINGS TO DO

A constellation is a group of stars which form a shape in the sky. Can you find the names of 6 constellations below?

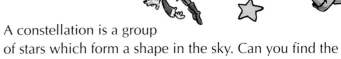

CORVUSTAURUSCYGNUSLEOURSAMAJORORION

How can you see flying saucers?

Trip up the waiter.

FILM SET FROLICS

DID YOU KNOW?

The first feature film ever was made in Australia in 1906. It was called *The Story of The Kelly Gang*.

1950's America saw the arrival of Smellovision or Aromarama, where appropriate smells were piped into seats during the film.

The biggest cinema in the world is the Radio City Music Hall in New York City. It has 5,874 seats.

THINGS TO DO

In this puzzle you are looking for 6 six-letter words to do with films. Each sentence below gives you a clue and 3 of the letters can be found in the boxes.

1. A film is shown on one.
2. A film is made with one.
3. Lipstick and powder.
4. A film is shown at one.
5. An actor learns his lines from one.
6. They make sure it's bright enough.

1. c r n
2. m c a 3. k a p
4. m i n 5. c s t 6. h i s

What's on at the cinema every week?

The roof.

I'D BE SURPRISED IF ANY FILMS WERE MADE IN SILLYWOOD STUDIOS, WOULDN'T YOU? AND AS IF THERE WASN'T ENOUGH CHAOS ALREADY, I CAN SEE SOMETHING ABOUT TO CAUSE MORE: IT'S YELLOW AND DANGEROUS DOWN ON THE FLOOR, WHEN THE MAN TAKES A STEP HE'LL GO FLYING FOR SURE.

CAN YOU MATCH THE SILHOUETTES TO THE RIGHT BITS IN THE PICTURE AND FIND THE ODD ONE OUT?

HI THERE, WIZARD WALLY-HUNTERS, THIS CONJURING SHOW HAS GOT OUT OF HAND. CAN YOU FIND 18 RIOTOUS RABBITS THAT HAVE BEEN PULLED OUT OF THE HAT? AND APART FROM ME, CAN YOU FIND THIS PERSON? SHE LOOKS ALARMED AND WOULDN'T YOU, HER LEGS HAVE LEFT HER IN A BOX SPOTTED BLUE.

WHICH OF THESE SILHOUETTES MATCHES THE MAGICIAN'S BUNNY?

A B C D E

MAGIC MAYHEM

DID YOU KNOW?

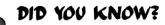

The fastest magician in the world is an American called Dr Eldoonie. He performed 118 different tricks in 2 minutes.

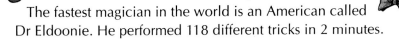

Harry Houdini was famous at the turn of the century for his great feats of escape. In a typical trick he would escape from being chained up and locked in a weighted and roped box that was thrown overboard from a boat. There was no magic involved in his escapes – just physical strength and great agility.

THINGS TO DO

Here's a magic number trick to try on your friends. You might need a calculator.
Pick a 2 digit number (2 different digits, like 84).
Reverse it (48).
Subtract the smaller number from the larger (84 – 48 = 36).
Divide this number by the difference between your original digits (36 ÷ 4). The final answer is always 9.

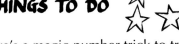

  What do you call a space magician?  *A flying sorceror.*

GREEN FOREST GAMES

DID YOU KNOW?

The first trees grew on Earth 280 million years ago.

The fastest growing tree in the world is the Eucalyptus. It can grow 3 cm in a day.

The slowest growing tree is the Sitka Spruce in the Arctic Circle. It can take 98 years to grow 28 cm.

THINGS TO DO

Grow your own trees.
Fill some small flower pots with potting compost and stand the pots in saucers. Collect pips from an orange, lemon or grapefruit and push them into the soil about 1 cm down – 1 pip per pot. Keep them in a warm, light place and water them frequently. As the seedlings get bigger, you may have to put them in bigger pots. You will never have fruit, but they look pretty and sometimes the leaves smell strongly.

What tree do hands grow on?   *A palm tree.*

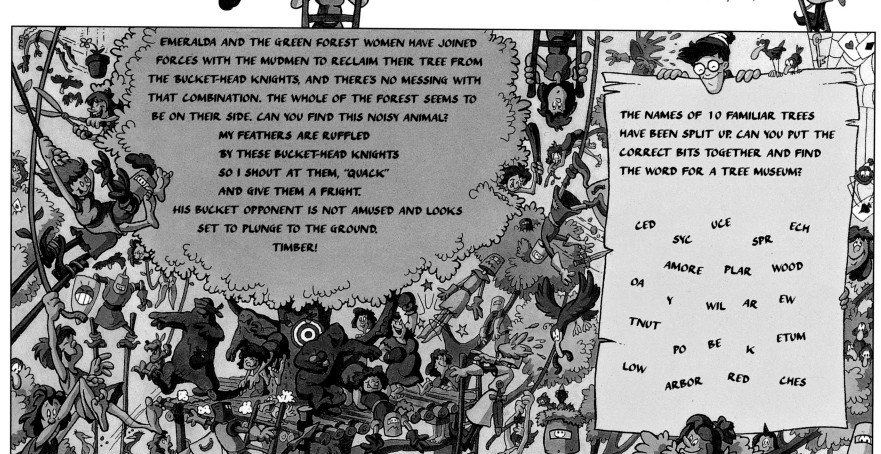

EMERALDA AND THE GREEN FOREST WOMEN HAVE JOINED FORCES WITH THE MUDMEN TO RECLAIM THEIR TREE FROM THE BUCKET-HEAD KNIGHTS, AND THERE'S NO MESSING WITH THAT COMBINATION. THE WHOLE OF THE FOREST SEEMS TO BE ON THEIR SIDE. CAN YOU FIND THIS NOISY ANIMAL?

MY FEATHERS ARE RUFFLED
BY THESE BUCKET-HEAD KNIGHTS
SO I SHOUT AT THEM, "QUACK"
AND GIVE THEM A FRIGHT.
HIS BUCKET OPPONENT IS NOT AMUSED AND LOOKS
SET TO PLUNGE TO THE GROUND.
TIMBER!

THE NAMES OF 10 FAMILIAR TREES HAVE BEEN SPLIT UP. CAN YOU PUT THE CORRECT BITS TOGETHER AND FIND THE WORD FOR A TREE MUSEUM?

CED   UCE   ECH
  SYC   SPR
    AMORE   PLAR   WOOD
OA
    Y   WIL   AR   EW
TNUT
      PO   BE   K   ETUM
LOW
  ARBOR   RED   CHES

WATER WONDERLAND

DID YOU KNOW?

Some seaweeds produce a sticky substance called alginic acid which helps them hold on to rocks. We add it to ice-cream to stop it separating.

The earliest submarines were powered by steam and got very hot under the water.

 One of the first submarines was used in 1776, during the American Civil War. It was called The Turtle.

THINGS TO DO

The message Wally has to find is written in code. Decode it by writing each set of letters down backwards.

LAWOT CODYL OTEMO OLAET TCOEV SUPO

Why did the crab blush? *Because the seaweed.*

DOG DAYS

DID YOU KNOW?

A dog called Braeburns's Close Encounter held the record for the most "Best in Show" awards. He won 203.

The biggest litter of any dog was 23 puppies, born to an American fox-hound called Lena.

There are over 400 species of dog in the world.

Unjumble the dog breeds below and fit them into the grid to find out who eventually won the show.

RITERER   MORDBEAN

HOEDSPEG

LANSPIE

SLATAINA   DRABAROL

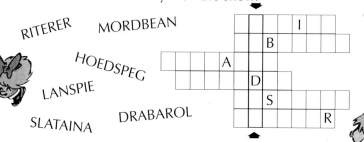

Grid letters: I, B, A, D, S, R

What did the dog say when he sat on a piece of sandpaper?   *Ruff!*

PHEW! THIS CHAOS SHOULD GIVE YOU
PAWS FOR THOUGHT. I WOULDN'T WANT
TO JUDGE THIS COMPETITION, ANYWAY
IT MIGHT BE A LITTLE DIFFICULT NOW.
  THE COVER IS GREEN
  ITS UP IN THE AIR
  ITS FULL OF THE RULES
  TO MAKE SURE
        THE SHOWS FAIR.
  TIME FOR ME TO TAKE
    MY BOW.

CAN YOU TELL WHERE
THESE 4 PICTURES COME FROM
IN THIS SCENE?

LIGHT FANTASTIC

DID YOU KNOW?

The light bulb was invented by Thomas Edison in 1879. Edison was responsible for lots of inventions, including a gramophone, a megaphone and a sewing machine that was run by the sound of a human voice.

1 square centimetre of the sun's surface is as bright as the light on 232,500 candles.

Each bulb at the top of the Empire State Building gives out the light of 450 million candles.

THINGS TO DO

The vanishing stamp trick
Here is a trick of the light. Put a postage stamp face up on the table. Put a glass of water on top of the stamp and a plate on top of the glass. Look into the glass from any angle and you will see that the stamp has disappeared.

What would you use if you swallowed a light bulb?

A candle.

THE VIKINGS

THE VIKINGS WERE GREAT
WARRIORS OF THE 9TH AND 11TH
CENTURIES, WHO RAIDED MANY COUNTRIES.
ON THIS GRID ARE THE NAMES OF 6 PLACES
THE VIKINGS INVADED. CAN YOU SPOT THEM ALL?

```
G P O I F U V S
R S B S R D O H
E N G L A N D E
E T R P N C D T
N O C O C A G L
L L H T E T E A
A M L F A L P N
N R U S S I A D
D N A L E R I S
```

DID YOU KNOW?

The Vikings sometimes gave their swords names and passed them down through the generations.

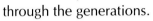

Different classes of Viking society worshipped different gods. The chieftains looked to Odin, and the freemen and women to Thor. The slaves were thought too lowly to have a god.

Some Vikings were buried in graves which were outlined with stones set in a boat shape.

THINGS TO DO

Can you match the silhouettes to the correct part of the picture? 2 shapes come from other scenes in the book.
Can you find which ones?

What did the Vikings use for secret messages?   Norse code.

CRAZY CARS

- A monkey
- A helicopter
- 2 arrows
- A piece of cake
- A purple balloon
- A parachute
- A dog in a balloon
- A grasshopper
- 3 green fish
- A snail

MOON WALKING

- 2 dogs in spacesuits
- A magnifying glass
- A pancake being tossed
- A chicken in a spacesuit
- A fish in a spacesuit
- 2 butterfly nets
- A snake in a spacesuit
- 3 smiling stars
- A satellite dish
- A baseball

MONSTER CARNIVAL

- A very thin clown
- 3 green buttons
- 2 pairs of glasses
- A striped parasol
- A green balloon
- A blue and white streamer
- Twin monster insects
- A question mark hat
- 10 Wally bobble hats
- A red bow tie

SURFER'S PARADISE

- 11 messages in bottles
- 2 swimming bears
- A pirate
- 3 pairs of goggles
- A bird in a nest
- A walrus
- A skier
- A raft racer
- A surfing dolphin
- 2 snorkellers

BALL SPORTS

- 19 tennis balls
- A broken tennis racket
- 2 striped balloons
- 2 flags
- A twisted golf club
- 4 coloured juggling balls
- 2 pool balls
- An orange balloon
- A huge bowling ball
- A man with a grey beard

FABULOUS FOOD

- 2 cherry cakes
- The chef
- A candle
- 3 carrots
- A bone
- A string of sausages
- 6 forks
- A banana
- A pickled gherkin
- A salt cellar

SHOPPING SPREE

- 11 red apples
- 7 bananas
- A boy eating chocolate
- 2 thermometers
- A yellow and white scarf
- A pillow
- A pink bow
- An octopus
- 2 pairs of square glasses
- A baby's bottle

MONKEY MISCHIEF

- 9 bananas
- A drawing of a sheep
- A striped parachute
- A broom
- A yellow striped hat
- A crashed purple plane
- 3 firemen
- A blue and white shirt
- A flying saucer
- 4 blue scarves

FLYING SAUCERS

- A man with 6 arms
- A green cat
- A flower
- 3 teacups
- 3 milk bottles
- A dog in a spacesuit
- A piece of cheese
- A cat in a spacesuit
- A slice of cake
- 3 mice

GREEN FOREST GAMES

- A plant in a pot
- 2 woodpeckers
- A key
- 2 men on stilts
- A Tarzan dog
- 2 boxing gloves
- A worm
- A pair of shears
- 3 playing cards
- A spider

LIGHT FANTASTIC

- A desk lamp hat
- 2 yellow headlamps
- A yellow Chinese lantern
- A man in a Wally lampshade
- An Aladdin's lamp
- A breaking fluorescent tube
- A pair of square glasses
- A brown book
- 9 candles
- 8 smiling light bulbs

FILM SET FROLICS

- A yellow bird
- A piece of cake
- 2 gold coins
- A sleeping man
- 3 men tangled in wires
- An umbrella
- 2 microphones
- A stills photographer
- An elephant
- A guitar

WATER WONDERLAND

- A starfish rowing a boat
- An orange balloon
- An upside-down craft
- A periscope
- A diver directing traffic
- A smiling torpedo
- A starfish riding 2 seahorses
- A turtle with an oxygen tank
- A starfish in goggles
- 11 shrimps

THE VIKINGS

- A telescope
- A shark
- A walking-stick
- 2 nests
- A message in a bottle
- A pair of scissors
- A duck
- 2 crabs
- A skull
- 4 rubber rings

MAGIC MAYHEM

- A yellow and red wand
- 11 juggling balls
- 4 red playing cards
- A wizard in a red hat
- 4 blue playing cards
- 7 top hats
- A yellow bow tie
- A frog
- A sorceress
- 10 white cards

DOG DAYS

- 17 bones
- A yellow dog bowl
- A pink sock
- A gold ring
- A man with a white moustache
- A man in a hat
- A sausage
- A man in purple trousers
- A lady in a red bow
- A woman in a vase

ANSWERS

MONSTER CARNIVAL

Riddle: There is a pink monster riding a unicycle with a mushroom hat.

Ball F is slightly bigger.

B and D are from this page but A is from Light Fantastic and C from Ball Sports.

Misfit: Little hooded man from Ball Sports.

FABULOUS FOOD

Riddle: There is a large pumpkin just beneath the right-hand picture.

Bits A and D complete the plate.

The vegetables are beetroot, cucumber, tomatoes, mushroom, potatoes, radishes. Radishes and tomatoes can be seen in the picture.

Misfit: White dog from Dog Days.

CRAZY CARS

Riddle: There is a baby in a blue pram next to the orange hippo.

Misfit: Bird from Green Forest Games.

SURFER'S PARADISE

Riddle: He's a teddy bear in Dracula's coffin on the far right of the picture.

The key and the anchor are the odd ones out because they do not float.

If you follow all the instructions you should end up in the Pacific.

Misfit: Fish from Water Wonderland.

SHOPPING SPREE

Riddle: He's looking for a slice of cheese next to the man with a cold.

Wally wanted to buy A Big Chocolate Cake.

Misfit: Top hat from Magic Mayhem.

MOON WALKING

Riddle: There are 14 little green men hiding in the picture.

The planets are: Mercury, Pluto, Saturn, Uranus, Jupiter, Mars, Earth, Venus, Neptune.

The space fact is: Neil Armstrong was the first man on the moon.

Misfit: Messy face from Fabulous Food.

BALL SPORTS

Riddle: The man at the front has put his finger through the hole in a table tennis bat.

The pool ball and tennis ball.

The sports are: basketball, football, tennis, swimming, golf, baseball, snooker, volleyball.

Swimming is the odd one – it's not a ball sport.

Misfit: Ribbon from Monster Carnival.

MONKEY MISCHIEF

Riddle: There is a man with a knife and fork and a potato up on the left.

Plane C matches exactly.

The animals are: tiger, mouse, zebra, camel, whale, horse, chimp, panda, sheep, hyena.

Misfit: Explorer from Film Set Frolics.

FLYING SAUCERS

Riddle: To the left of Wally's spaceship is a spaceman floating upside down who has dropped his ice-cream.

The constellations are:
Corvus – the crow, Taurus – the bull, Cygnus – the swan, Leo – the lion, Ursa Major – the great bear, Orion – the hunter.

Misfit: Pilot from Monkey Mischief.

FILM SET FROLICS

Riddle: The man Tarzan is looking at is about to step on a banana skin.

The film words are: 1. Screen 2. Camera 3. Makeup 4. Cinema 5. Script 6. Lights.

The kangaroo head is from Crazy Cars.

Misfit: Sunbather from Surfer's Paradise.

MAGIC MAYHEM

Riddle: A woman has been sawn in half under the huge pink rabbit.

Silhouette E matches the bunny.

Misfit: Light bulb from Light Fantastic.

GREEN FOREST GAMES

Riddle: There is a yellow duck standing on the tree house.

The trees are cedar, yew, redwood, spruce, chestnut, poplar, sycamore, beech, willow, oak, and the tree museum is an arboretum.

Misfit: Helmet from The Vikings.

WATER WONDERLAND

Riddle: There is a message in a bottle on the rock in the middle of the picture.

The coded message reads: To Wally, do come to tea, Love Octopus.

Misfit: Spaceship from Moon Walking.

DOG DAYS

Riddle: There is a little green rule book at the top of the page.

Misfit: Little girl from Shopping Spree.

LIGHT FANTASTIC

Riddle: Man cooking a sausage over a lamp.

Lamp D is missing from the picture.

Misfit: Space car from Flying Saucers.

THE VIKINGS

Riddle: A Viking is cleaning the helmets on the head of the long boat.

Helmet C is the odd one out.

The dragon is from Surfer's Paradise and the chicken in a spacesuit from Moon Walking.

Misfit: Child's face from Crazy Cars.

AND FINALLY

Wenda, Whitebeard, Woof and Odlaw are in Crazy Cars. Whitebeard is also in Magic Mayhem and Woof is in Flying Saucers. The scrolls are in Monkey Mischief, Film Set Frolics and The Vikings, and the Wally flag is in The Vikings.

With special thanks to Stephen Martiniere and Greg Dubuque.

First published 1994 by Walker Books Ltd
87 Vauxhall Walk, London SE11 5HJ
This edition published 2009
1 2 3 4 5 6 7 8 9 10
Text © 1994 Martin Handford
The right of Martin Handford to be identified as author/illustrator of this work has been asserted by him in accordance with the Copyright, Designs and Patents Act 1988
This book has been typeset in Optima
Printed in China
All rights reserved.
British Library Cataloguing in Publication Data:
a catalogue record for this book is available from the British Library
ISBN: 978-1-4063-2375-7
www.walker.co.uk

The facts in this book were correct for the first publication in 1994